JANE WILSON

Jane Wilson

LAND | SEA | SKY

Interview by Justin Spring

Introduction by Anne Cohen DePietro

Photographs by John Jonas Gruen

DC Moore Gallery

Heckscher Museum of Art

Nature as Event: The Art of Jane Wilson

Lately, driving in late afternoon as the sun begins to dim in the west, I've been seeing Jane Wilson skies. October was notable this year for its mild temperatures, clear weather, and spectacular sunsets. Late-day drifts of clouds would trail ever so slowly across the heavens. As a large roseate sun gradually worked its way to the horizon, the sky would suffuse with incredibly intense bands of pink, purple, and coral set against a deep blue slowly fading to plum-gray—sunsets in Technicolor, so exquisite they defy description. They are Jane Wilson sunsets, hovering above the landscape and waterways of Long Island that have long informed her work.

In Iowa, where Jane Wilson was born and raised, life has always revolved around the weather. Wilson recounts how, in midwestern farm country, changing weather conditions and storms were greeted with excitement. When people met, they would discuss storms as though shared events. In agricultural communities, where weather dictates the success or failure of crops and tornadoes are not uncommon, such a phenomenon is hardly surprising. This uniquely midwestern experience left Wilson with a strong attachment to the ephemeral qualities of changing weather and an appreciation of nature as event.

Jane Wilson's paintings, too, are events, celebrating the times of day, the seasons, and the weather. They are light-infused compositions, in which nature is at center stage. Whether a midnight-blue sky dimly illuminated by a small crescent moon, as in *Midnight Clear*, or a chill, pellucid dawn of the palest pinks and yellows, or a baroque confection of a sunset as brilliant as a Tiepolo sky, Wilson manages to convey the precise climatic conditions of a moment. Damp fog, the threat of torrential rain in a swirl of wind-tossed clouds, and the frigid chill of winter—all are described with equal facility. Nature is alternately tranquil and serene or intensely dramatic, but always worthy of contemplation.

Her painting is as much about place and a recalled sense of experience as it is about method. "The place is everything as far as I'm concerned."[1] Indeed, her earliest memories of her Iowa childhood are of the expanses of flat terrain, the western sunsets of red and gold, and the weather. After traditional Sunday dinners, Jane and her sister were taken by their parents on long afternoon drives to the Mississippi River, whose vast expanses of water left an indelible impression of astonishment and mystery.

To stand before a landscape by Jane Wilson is to experience a quiet ecstasy, and wonder at the extraordinarily ephemeral light, radiant color, and palpable atmosphere contained therein. Resolutely contemporary in its pared-down composition of bands of color, and its candid acknowledgment of the flat pictorial plane, Wilson's painting nonetheless shares with nineteenth-century landscape painting elements of transcendental idealism and romanticism. The dramatic sunsets of J. M. W. Turner and Thomas Moran, the ethereal moonrings of Edward Steichen, and the sublime seascapes of Fitz Hugh Lane come to mind as kindred celebrations of nature. The cool northern light of Dutch and German landscape and the scintillating color, broken brushstroke, and diffuse form of French Impressionism equally inform Wilson's paintings. Yet her work is truly about the act of art-making, and about a method of working that gradually intuits place, time of day, and condition of weather.

1. Conversation with Jane Wilson, New York City, September 20, 2000.

While they bear titles allusive to the east end of Long Island, where she and her husband, John Jonas Gruen, have had a country home since the late 1950s, Wilson's landscapes could be from anywhere. With sweeping vistas of bayfronts and potato fields and a rush of clouds overhead, they are nature in microcosm. Universal landscapes, they share characteristics with Iowa farmland, the Mississippi delta, and other destinations; this past summer Wilson was in Brittany, in St. Malo, where she was enchanted by the ever-changing weather patterns. She does most of her painting in her New York City studio, drawing upon recalled sensations and experience.

Wilson never begins a painting with a preconceived idea of what the image will be, but the horizon line is always low. The basic format is consistent, yet it varies significantly from one painting to the next; it is never formulaic. Several horizontal bands delineate horizon and, possibly, strips of light, land, and water. The undercoat is important; it provides the internal light of the painting and dictates what will follow. She always works from the top of the canvas downward, with a limited range of colors. Layer upon layer of pigment—as many as thirty to a painting—are added to provide translucence. Wilson typically works with one complementary tone over another; she is an extraordinary colorist. The layers create an optical mix, causing her canvases to resonate with light. Hers is an approach to painting that has evolved from doing and from studying the work of others; it is not something that can be learned at school. Painting wet over dry, Wilson follows an unhurried and instinctive process, one that descends from the abstract expressionism that dominated the art scene when she first moved to New York, in 1950. Even in the heyday of that movement, her work was always about landscape, and about still life.

Jane Wilson's paintings are what an artist I know calls "stare pictures." To be surrounded by them in a gallery is an absorbing and even sensuous experience. Works such as *American Horizon* and *Black Wind* literally take one's breath away. A dean of American painting, Jane Wilson speaks about her work with grace and clarity and is deeply interested in the work of other artists. With a master's degree in painting and a passion for art history, she pursues their work and seeks out examples in museum collections and in books. Indeed, much of what she has learned about painting comes from looking at, and studying, the work of others, spanning the Renaissance down to the present. She is drawn to the work of northern European painters and has been influenced by the cool blue light that filters through their landscapes. Her own work, truly a celebration of nature as event, is equally the summation of a lifetime of thoughtful looking, of memory, experience, and reflection.

The present exhibition at the Heckscher Museum of Art, in encompassing her current work as well as a broad overview of paintings created since 1993, celebrates the exquisite art and remarkable vision of Jane Wilson.

—Anne Cohen DePietro
Chief Curator, Heckscher Museum of Art

It has been a great pleasure to work with the artist, Suzanne Julig, and Bridget Moore of DC Moore Gallery, as well as John Jonas Gruen, who has so generously lent a selection of his wonderful photographs of Jane.

A Conversation with Jane Wilson

by Justin Spring

Jane Wilson has had a distinguished fifty-year career as a painter and teacher of painting. She is an engaging conversationalist and a graceful public speaker, but has never before been interviewed in print about her life and work. Her reticence is something she credits, naturally enough, to her midwestern upbringing; as she explains, people who live on farms tend to be visually observant but cautious with words. And, indeed, an understanding of her midwestern background is crucial to an understanding of her art.

Born on a small family farm outside Seymour, Iowa, Wilson had a peripatetic early life. During the Depression, her father gave up farming to work for the state highway commission, which meant the family relocated frequently, moving through a series of Iowa farming towns until Wilson reached college age. With her father absent much of the time, she and her younger sister, Ann, grew up on farms that were essentially run by their mother, an enterprising woman who had started out as a schoolteacher and art student but became a novelist and poet, and who, at age fifty, returned to the University of Iowa to get an M.A. in political science.

Circumspection and forbearance are essential to the confines and isolation of farm life, as are stoicism, resilience, and a quiet sense of humor. These qualities have served Jane Wilson well, for the life of the artist is not unlike that of a farmer—full of uncertainty and financial hardship, requiring faith in one's own abilities, and, of course, working solitude.

Since moving to New York City in 1950, Wilson has exhibited steadily. A founding member of the Hansa Gallery Cooperative, she was part of a generation of artists who came of age in the wake of Abstract Expressionism—a loosely knit group known as the "Second Generation Abstract Expressionists." This group came to include artists as varied as Joan Mitchell, Fairfield Porter, Jan Muller, Wolf Kahn, and Larry Rivers.

Wilson supported herself during her early years in New York in a number of ways—clerking at a book store, working as a fashion model, and once even appearing on *The $64,000 Challenge* television show. She has taught at Pratt Art Institute, Cooper Union, Parsons School of Design, and, most recently, Columbia University, and has been named visiting artist at a number of colleges and universities around the country. She was president of the National Academy of Design, chair of the Skowhegan School of Painting and Sculpture, chair of the Columbia University art department, and a member of the American Academy of Arts and Letters since 1991. She resides with her husband of over fifty years, the writer and photographer John Gruen, on the Upper West Side of New York City, and they keep a house in Water Mill, on the east end of Long Island. They have a grown daughter, Julia.

Wilson recently joined me after a day in the studio to discuss her life and work at the DC Moore Gallery on Fifth Avenue, where twelve of her most recent paintings had been set out for us to enjoy.

Jane, while I'd like to talk about the whole of your career, I'll start by asking if there are any generalizations you can make about your paintings of the past ten years, from 1990–2000.

Well, I suppose I could say that during this time I realized for the nth time that landscape was the most natural or intuitive subject matter, or departure point, for my images, and so I have been pursuing it exclusively. Up until 1990 I had been working through different forms of subject matter, including still life.

Why abandon still life?

Still life offered a different kind of wholeness. Still life is indoor, tactile, and physical, about touch, texture, and weight, substance, and the intimate distances in between. And the idea came to me to work instead with subjects that have no palpable substance whatsoever, yet which we experience every day. Of course, my paintings have intimations of land and water, but really they're about the other part, the insubstantial part.

Where did this interest come from?

I was reading Arnheim...

... Rudolph Arnheim, the gestalt psychologist and aesthetician who wrote the book Art and Visual Perception *back in the fifties...*

Yes—I must admit to reading him belatedly!—and for me it was all about the substance of things without substance—our experience of the insubstantial being that which makes the insubstantial visible. That was when the idea of the painting as a "container of endless experience" became most appealing to me. And the most basic form for that idea was the sky.

You seem to have a basic form, or, to use a Jungian expression, archetype, in these works—the low-horizoned landscape.

Yes, I do. I feel that there's a geographic center and a gravity center in every canvas. Those are the very points that need to be actively "empty," but it's different for every artist. And this is mine—the low-horizoned landscape. It's basic to me, my basic form, leaning predominantly on the square.

Where do you think that form comes from?

I think there's a basic shape sense that dates from the time you first open your eyes. That evolves with you as you grow up. Then there's the great sense of freedom that comes to a child on first being allowed outside, for example, as a separate person in the world. Being out-of-doors is one of the most mysterious experiences on earth.

Can you tell me something about your family and early life?

Well, my father was from a large, very close-knit farm family, and I was born on a farm that had been given to him by his father. My father trained in civil engineering at Iowa State University in Ames. But, in his family, if children left or married "wrong," they were considered "bad." And I think in his family Dad was considered to have married "wrong." Eventually my parents divorced, and it was sad.

I was born April 29, 1924, the first of two girls, and had three years of my parents' undivided attention. My father would work outdoors until the end of the day and my mother was the housewife. A farm housewife's duties in those days included just about everything—she'd do the cooking, the cleaning, the canning, feed the chickens, tend the garden, slop the hogs, milk the cows, make the sausages…life was an unending preparation for all seasons and eventualities.

Were you looking at pictures much as a child?

Not really, but we had an oleograph of *Song of the Lark* and one of *The Angelus* in our living room.

Studying art in school?

I took an art course in high school—what was offered. But there really wasn't much. I used to copy those "Draw Me!" ads on the back of matchbooks. [Laughs] And I copied cartoons and photographs of movie stars. I had a whole scrapbook of movie stars.

No landscapes?

No landscapes. Only faces, and horses, and medieval princesses. I loved being out of doors, though. Restlessness was taken care of by going across the railroad tracks to a wonderful open woods. So being out of doors was…well, I think it cured everything.

You had a good, solid education as an artist at the University of Iowa.

Yes. When I arrived, Grant Wood had just left, and the new head was a man named Lester Longman from Columbia University. He had arrived with a number of artists from New York, including Mary Holmes, who is the most brilliant lecturer I have ever heard, and James Lechay, the teacher who affected me most directly—he's now alive and well and exhibiting at something like 90. They were all fresh out of New York and really immersed in the international art world of the time. Also, when Dr. Longman came in, the University decided it was going to make a really first-rate art school, with art history taught to suit the needs of the art student rather than the art historian. And so the faculty there were artists who were actually exhibiting…and students were seeing the idea of how you prepare for a life in art. It was all very innovative.

What was the transition like, moving to New York?

Well, I came to New York with my M.A. in painting and two years of teaching art history at Iowa

and that false sense of accomplishment that a graduate student has. I felt it would be smart to go to Hans Hofmann's School and work there for a while. But I found I could not go near a classroom again.... Still, just about every artist I knew had studied with Hans Hofmann. But I've never been very good at joining groups, and so I never studied with him.

One of the big social centers for the art world of the time was the Cedar Tavern.

Yes, we went there. I went to my job in the daytime—first at a bookshop, then later, modelling, for which some people will never forgive me—then back home to paint, until about 11pm, and afterward we would go out to the Cedar Tavern for an hour or so. It was part of our routine.

What was your life like, starting out?

Well, we moved every six months... It was always a rented room, that kind of situation. It was very borderline. We had very little income. Nobody did. And something midwestern in me couldn't deal with the anxiety of not having money enough to be able to... somebody had to have a job. It's in my character. I have to be able to provide for myself and my studio. So I worked.

Willem de Kooning, Jane Wilson and daughter Julia Gruen (age 4), Water Mill, New York, 1962

Were you selling any paintings?

Yes, actually, little ones, all along. It began when John worked at Brentano's… There was a woman he met there who sort of adopted us. We were very adoptable—fresh-eyed and fresh out of graduate school—and she would pay me $25 to do some small paintings. Those sorts of sales, that kind of encouragement, was crucial. Very, very important. Fairfield [Porter] helped in another way, being very supportive and genuinely interested in my work. And there were also people who sort of liked the idea that we were living the dream.

Were you dropping by The Club, the Abstract Expressionists' meeting-place on Eighth Street?

A little. You had to be invited, or at least I felt I did…it was a membership. I pressed my nose against the window. I mean, you could go, in theory, if somebody said "come." But I would never, with my background, go there without being specifically invited. Maybe others did, I don't know. I remember that the women tended to bustle around in the back, making coffee and serving food. Washing dishes. It was a little too church basement for me. My instinct led me to find my own way.

But you know, at a certain point Milton Resnick, who was one of the world's handsomest men, said, "Jane, I'd like to put you up for membership." It was at that point that I realized that I only wanted to be invited to the party—I didn't want to attend. [Laughs].

What was it like?

Oh, one-upmanship was all over the place. It was very entertaining, on a very silly level. Very gladiatorial. Mostly you went to see and hear Bill [de Kooning] or Pollock, or Rothko occasionally. But they all seemed very unapproachable to me.

Would you describe yourself, then, as a solitary person?

I would. The way I grew up…didn't encourage me to be outgoing. Neither of my parents were outgoing. Our life was solitary because that's how farm life is. And because we moved so much, we were always, in a sense, foreigners or aliens.

Would you say there was an emotional component to your flat, low landscapes?

Yes. I'd describe it as the experience of solitude. Growing up on a farm you accept solitude and live with it. Solitude is midwestern. It's not loneliness. It's solitude, and it's valuable.

And it's there in the paintings?

I think so. It's very basic to that landscape. Just as living close to nature is. Everyone on a farm is observant of nature—though not consciously in an aesthetic sense. On a farm, you're very aware of weather because so much of your life is dependent on it. And in a place like Iowa the weather can be so extreme. You learn to feel the weather coming. The animals do it as well. Weather is not just visual, you can feel it with all your senses. That's what I'd like to get at in my paintings—that full-body feeling. You sniff the weather, and a complicated rush of feeling runs through you.

I think I know what you mean. Whenever my dog goes outside, she lifts up her head up and gives a thoughtful sniff, as if deciding what kind of day it's going to be.

She's very wise! [Laughs] But you know, I think I'm like that, too—I think that there's some part of me that's very open and responsive to the atmosphere, that finds it an important or substantial experience. It's one of the reasons I like living on the Upper West Side, near the park and the river. You're more exposed to the weather up there.

Which brings us to an interesting point—you're a city person.

Yes. The unstaunchable energy of the city is addictive.

It seems paradoxical for a city person to paint flat horizons and wide-open skies.

Well, I once met a scholar, a brilliant scholar, who grew up on a farm in Tennessee, and I said to him, "I hear Tennessee is one of the most beautiful places on earth." And he nodded thoughtfully, and he said, "Only once you've left it." [Laughs] I guess I'm a bit like that.

But there's some basic life experience to the painting all the same?

Yes. And, you know, we have landscapes and skyscapes like this at our house in Water Mill. But I suppose one of the things I'm more and more conscious of is that there's a retinal experience of the outdoors I'm trying to get at—it's a retinal buzz that seems part of a very basic, intuitive experience. I try to find that retinal buzz in the colors of the painting.

With landscapes this simplified, the horizon line becomes very important.

Yes. The grand infinity out there, up above and down below.

What is your feeling about horizons—what do they mean to you?

I've always been fascinated by the horizon. As a child I felt pulled toward it—it pulled me into dreams. I felt that beyond the horizon was where my life was going to happen, was where my future lay. I think that's another very significant experience when you grow up on a farm in the Midwest—that you grow up feeling it's your destiny to leave, to see things, to wander.

So many people associate skies with feelings of transcendence or exaltation. Would you say that there is a spiritual element to your work?

That's a tricky question. I don't quite know how to answer it. I would say that painting is a meditative practice. And I would say that, if anything, I'm pantheistic in my spirituality. Artistic practice is

work—it's very focused and rigorous—and yet at the same time, doing it, you somehow get beyond immediate distractions, into something inner, deep and important … the under-self.

The painting I do is the only way I have to catch something that is constantly changing. To capture experience. Light has a physical presence, but at the same time it's fused into this magnetic experience of sky which is totally elusive. So there's a metaphorical element to this practice—the constant challenge of trying to capture something that can't be captured. I love how the sky is constantly changing, how it's so complicated. Changing color, changing humidity, changing light, changing winds, changing temperature. It's really too much to deal with! And yet, at the same time, I find the experience vital and elating.

And I do think that there's something universal in the experience of the sky, a feeling that truly envelops you. You see it in the Orant's posture—that early Christian prayer figure which holds up its hands to receive the blessing of the sky.

TOP ROW: Tibor De Nagy, Rudy Burckhardt, Roland Pease; MIDDLE ROW: Jane Wilson, Yvonne Jacquette, Jane Freilicher;

BOTTOM ROW: Arthur Gold, Robert Fizdale, Joe Hazan; Water Mill, New York, 1962

The 20th-century artist whose work fuses the abstract, the atmospheric, and the spiritual is Mark Rothko.

The first Rothko retrospective at MoMA had a very strong effect on me. I remember how, at MoMA, the paintings were hung very low and the rooms were dark and had an intimate scale. And it was a revelation. There's a mastery in his work that is breathtaking. His awareness of scale and geometric physicalities. He just had it. You find genius like that strewn through history, in Piero, for instance, and Pisanello and Turner. And it goes back further, to relief sculpture, as the basis for form in painting. But Rothko definitely had that spacial and physical awareness.

You've spoken before about the importance of sculpture and bas-relief to your understanding of painting. Can you give me an example?

Ghiberti's Baptistery doors in Florence are probably the best example. Over and over again, those reliefs are departure points into the purely pictorial. They are like paintings that come and get you and pull you into their world. That's my idea of great art—it comes out and gets you and pulls you in.

I know that you admire de Kooning.

Yes. He had been trained academically and earned his way out by knowing his stuff. I admired that, and his gesture, and the breadth of the color passages, and the choppy line…those images stayed with me. Liking or disliking began to seem irrelevant, it's whether the image stays with you that's important. At least, that's the understanding I came to…probably in the mid-fifties or so.

At the same time, I knew I couldn't go in that direction. I was probably more interested in people like Braque, and Kline. Kline's gesture. There is a strong ingredient of value-play in Kline, and it took many years for me to get into that and disentangle it.

There's a landscape quality to his work.

Yes, I think so. Landscapes and citiscapes. He's from Wilkes Barre. I went there once, and I was told that under the city there are coal mines, many coal mines, and that they're on fire, burning and unquenchable…what an image!

But with Kline there was also the el [the elevated subway], and I think there's a lot of the el in his work.

It seems to me that besides being well acquainted with the Abstract Expressionists, you were also influenced by the Intimist Painters—the French Post-Impressionists Vuillard and Bonnard, who were being shown at MoMA in the late forties and fifties—and by the other young artists around you who were also caught up in the ideas of the Intimist painters.

Yes. I've thought about Vuillard and Bonnard quite a bit. In fact, I think what I'm doing in my painting is creating an experience of largeness in landscape from an Intimist's point of view…that's what I've tried to reconcile: the largeness and the intimacy. That paradox.

Are there other contemporary artists whose work has influenced you?

Many. So many it would be impossible to name them.

Could you name just a few?

[Reluctantly] Well…Diebenkorn, for his ability to project the thickness of light, the quality of light and air. Guston, because his paintings have a real physicality. He gets to feeling through pigment. Joan Mitchell, because you can feel nature through her paintings. Jane Freilicher—I wish I had her wonderful liquidity of image. Fairfield [Porter], of course…Albert York is a unique artist in the vein of [Albert Pinkham] Ryder, and I think Lois Dodd is a greatly underrated landscape painter. Her work to me is almost sculptural. There is Jim Nutt, in Chicago, with his hypnotically intense color in his small paintings of heads. But there are many, many others.

Would you say that, in order to get to that sense of drama or engagement you just mentioned, you tend to focus on moments of change in weather?

Yes, I do. But I'm also fascinated by moments of absolute stillness, those moments when we are just hypnotized by stillness. What I'm aiming for are moments of strong sensation—moments of total physical experience of landscape, when the weather just reaches out and sucks you in. And the challenge of trying to trigger those moments with pigments of ground-up earth. When you think about it, it's really very mysterious.

Mysterious enough to return to it over and over again.

Yes. Joshua Reynolds, when asked about a finished portrait, said, "Underneath are many versions, some better, some worse." That just about says it all, I think. Certainly for me.

When you work in the same form over and over again, the challenge has to be in finding some way to keep the challenge up, to keep the game going.

Yes. I sometimes wonder whether I can do it. But then I go to the canvas, and a certain kind of ritual begins.

Do you work on one canvas at a time?

Oh, no! [Laughs] I keep many. With each painting I'm trying to find the door rather than the wall. Sometimes it takes a while. Sometimes after a year you can look at a painting and see the problem immediately. And you wonder why you ever got stuck.

How can you tell when a painting is working?

I've learned through the years, through self-education, that there are many ways of reading a painting. There's a book by Eastlake, published in two volumes in about 1825, which I bought about thirty-five years ago. The book is about portraits, but the ideas in it are magnificent. Mid-way through the second volume the word abstract appears over and over again. It turns out that all artists who received studio training at this time were taught to look for the abstract of the value structure. Which is completely different from the actual subject. Then you think of color—that's another layer of abstraction. And light is another layer. Which explains why a good painting is hard to analyze. Gainsborough, for instance, could make a rock-solid painting even when his subject is a lady who looks entirely ethereal. Reading through this book, I was able to make a catalogue of things that every artist could be aware of and use to find out what's not working. I applied it immediately to my own painting and I saw an immediate improvement. I now had a point of view! [Laughs] I could analyze my painting. It was a revelation to me. De Kooning had that ability from the very earliest; he walked in with it. But I had to come to it through self-education.

You don't seem overly concerned with literal transcription.

No. Literal transcription and plein air painting are not part of my work. I like an outdoor feeling in my work, but that's a different thing. Then again I don't think the Impressionists were all that concerned with literal transcription either. There are too many beautiful Sundays in those paintings—Paris doesn't always look like that. Anyone who has been drenched in the cold, windy rain of northern France can tell you that. So it's not literal transcription. What I'm trying to get at is a painting that gives you a strong sensation—so strong that you have an instinctual, confident assessment of a very particular moment of time and place and weather and season.

I remember once at an exhibition of my work there was a baby being carried through the gallery, and as it passed by one of my small paintings its eyes grew large and it pointed and said, "Moon." I think that was the greatest compliment my painting has ever received!

So you seem to be getting at something beyond the physical; some very real mystery that exists in everyday experience.

Yes. Something real. Like the weather. You can't touch it, you can't escape it. It's real.

Justin Spring is a novelist, critic, and art historian. His biography *Fairfield Porter: A Life in Art* was recently published. He has also written books on Jackson Pollock and Edward Hopper. Spring's articles on contemporary art, photography, literature, and design have appeared in *Artforum*, *ARTnews*, *The New York Times*, *The Village Voice*, and *Art & Text*.

WORKS IN THE EXHIBITION
HECKSCHER MUSEUM OF ART

AMERICAN HORIZON   2000, oil on linen, 66 x 77 inches   *(Private Collection)*

ANXIOUS WINDS   2000, oil on linen, 24 x 24 inches

BLACK WIND   2000, oil on linen, 84 x 70 inches   *(Private Collection)*

CHILLY DAWN: WATER MILL   2000, oil on linen, 24 x 24 inches

DAWN INTO DAY: NORTH HAVEN   2000, oil on linen, 38 x 50 inches   *(Private Collection)*

FOG-LIT NIGHT   2000, oil on linen, 18 x 18 inches

HOVERING FOG   2000, oil on linen, 30 x 36 inches

HUMID MIDNIGHT   2000, oil on linen, 18 x 18 inches

ICY DAY   2000, oil on linen, 30 x 36 inches   *(Private Collection)*

LIGHT AT DAWN   2000, oil on linen, 18 x 18 inches

LINGERING BLUE   2000, oil on linen, 60 x 60 inches

LONG WINTER EVENING: FLYING POINT   2000, oil on linen, 60 x 60 inches

MIDNIGHT CLEAR   2000, oil on linen, 18 x 18 inches

SPRING CHILL   2000, oil on linen, 24 x 24 inches

SUN IN FEBRUARY   2000, oil on linen, 38 x 50 inches

VANISHING MOON: WATER MILL   2000, oil on linen, 24 x 24 inches

EARLY ONE MORNING   1999, oil on linen, 24 x 24 inches

FOGGY NIGHT: SAGAPONACK   1999, oil on linen, 18 x 18 inches   *(Private Collection, Courtesy of Lizan Tops Gallery)*

MID-AFTERNOON STORM   1999, oil on linen, 18 x 18 inches

SAGAPONACK MORNING   1999, oil on linen, 36 x 36 inches

SLEEPING MOON   1999, oil on linen, 18 x 18 inches

ANOTHER SPRING   1998, oil on linen, 55 x 60 inches

HAZE AT DAWN   1998, oil on linen, 18 x 18 inches

MARCH WIND: WATER MILL   1998, oil on linen, 60 x 60 inches

AT DAWN   1997, oil on linen, 38 x 50 inches

DARKNESS   1997, oil on linen, 60 x 60 inches

GREEN PALISADE   1997, oil on linen, 30 x 36 inches

PALISADE AT MIDNIGHT   1997, oil on linen, 24 x 24 inches

RAINFALL   1997, oil on linen, 18 x 18 inches

SEPTEMBER NIGHT   1997, oil on linen, 84 x 70 inches   *(Collection of Julia Gruen)*

STORM IN TRANSIT   1997, oil on linen, 24 x 24 inches

NIGHT AT MECOX CUT   1996, oil on linen, 14 x 16 inches

CLEAR DAY AT FLYING POINT   1995, oil on linen, 70 x 78 inches   *(Collection of the Artist)*

REMEMBERED DAY: PECONIC   1995, oil on linen, 18 x 18 inches

SALT MARSH   1993, oil on linen, 70 x 60 inches

SEPTEMBER SECOND: WATER MILL   1993, oil on linen, 80 x 70 inches

All works courtesy of DC Moore Gallery, unless otherwise noted.

AMERICAN HORIZON 2000, oil on linen, 66 x 77 inches

ANXIOUS WINDS   2000, oil on linen, 24 x 24 inches

CHILLY DAWN: WATER MILL   2000, oil on linen, 24 x 24 inches

DAWN INTO DAY: NORTH HAVEN   2000, oil on linen, 38 x 50 inches

HOVERING FOG   2000, oil on linen, 30 x 36 inches

LIGHT AT DAWN   2000, oil on linen, 18 x 18 inches

MIDNIGHT CLEAR   2000, oil on linen, 18 x 18 inches

ICY DAY   2000, oil on linen, 30 x 36 inches

HUMID MIDNIGHT   2000, oil on linen, 18 x 18 inches

FOG-LIT NIGHT   2000, oil on linen, 18 x 18 inches

LINGERING BLUE   2000, oil on linen, 60 x 60 inches

LONG WINTER EVENING: FLYING POINT 2000, oil on linen, 60 x 60 inches

SPRING CHILL   2000, oil on linen, 24 x 24 inches

VANISHING MOON: WATER MILL   2000, oil on linen, 24 x 24 inches

SUN IN FEBRUARY 2000, oil on linen, 38 x 50 inches

SLEEPING MOON   1999, oil on linen, 18 x 18 inches

FOGGY NIGHT: SAGAPONACK 1999, oil on linen, 18 x 18 inches

MID-AFTERNOON STORM   1999, oil on linen, 18 x 18 inches

SAGAPONACK MORNING   1999, oil on linen, 36 x 36 inches

MARCH WIND: WATER MILL   1998, oil on linen, 60 x 60 inches

DARKNESS   1997, oil on linen, 60 x 60 inches

AT DAWN   1997, oil on linen, 38 x 50 inches

GREEN PALISADE   1997, oil on linen, 30 x 36 inches

STORM IN TRANSIT 1997, oil on linen, 24 x 24 inches

PALISADE AT MIDNIGHT   1997, oil on linen, 24 x 24 inches

RAINFALL   1997, oil on linen, 18 x 18 inches

SEPTEMBER NIGHT   1997, oil on linen, 84 x 70 inches

NIGHT AT MECOX CUT   1996, oil on linen, 14 x 16 inches

CLEAR DAY AT FLYING POINT 1995, oil on linen, 70 x 78 inches

SALT MARSH   1993, oil on linen, 70 x 60 inches

SEPTEMBER SECOND: WATER MILL   1993, oil on linen, 80 x 70 inches

JANE WILSON

Master Works — Modern and Contemporary, Marianne Friedland Gallery, Naples, FL

Re-presenting Representation, Arnot Art Museum, Elmira, NY

Still Life 1963–1993, Gerald Peters Gallery, Santa Fe, NM, organized by John Arthur

1992

Elemental Nature, Midtown Payson Galleries, New York, NY

New Viewpoints: Contemporary American Women Realists, Consular Residence, Universal Exposition, Seville, Spain; developed by The National Museum of Women in the Arts, Washington, DC

1991–92

On Tabletop and Wall: The Art of the American Still Life, Pennsylvania Academy of the Fine Arts, Philadelphia, PA

American Realism & Figurative Art: 1952– 1991, organized by John Arthur and the Japan Association of Art Museums *(traveled to: The Miyagi Museum of Art, Sendai; Sojo Museum of Art, Yokohama; The Tokushima Modern Art Museum, Tokushima; The Museum of Modern Art, Shiba; Otsu Kochi Prefectural Museum of Folk Art, Kochi)*

1991

Beyond the Picturesque: Landscapes on Paper, G.W. Einstein Company, New York, NY

Exquisite and Sublime, New Jersey Center for Visual Arts, Summit, NJ

Urban Icons, Klarfeld Perry Gallery, New York, NY

1990

A Little Night Music — Manhattan in the Dark, Lintas Worldwide, One Dag Hammarskjold Plaza, New York, NY, curated by Gerrit Henry

40th Anniversary Exhibition, Tibor de Nagy Gallery, New York, NY

Horizons, General Electric Company, Stamford, CT, organized by the Art Advisory Service of the Museum of Modern Art, New York, NY

Long Island Landscape Painting in the Twentieth Century, Heckscher Museum of Art, Huntington, NY

The 1950s at the Tibor de Nagy Gallery, LaGuardia Hall, Brooklyn College, Brooklyn, NY

The Painterly Landscape, C. Grimaldis Gallery, Baltimore, MD

1989–91

At the Water's Edge: 19th and 20th Century American Beach Scenes, Tampa Museum of Art, Tampa, FL *(traveled to: Center for the Arts, Vero Beach, FL; Virginia Beach Center for the Arts, Virginia Beach, VA; The Arkansas Arts Center, Little Rock, AR)*

1989–90

Documenting a Moment: Contemporary Plein Air Landscape, Tatistcheff Gallery, Santa Monica, CA

1989

American Art Today: Contemporary Landscape, The Art Museum, Florida International University, Miami, FL

Artist/Photographer/Artist, Benton Gallery, Southampton, NY

Contemporary Environment, General Electric Company, Stamford, CT, organized by the Art Advisory Service of the Museum of Modern Art, New York, NY

The Food Show, Grand Central Art Galleries, New York, NY

June Moon, G.W. Einstein Company, New York, NY

The Natural Image, Stamford Museum and Nature Center, Stamford, CT

Neo-Romantics, Williams Center for the Arts, Lafayette College, Easton, PA, curated by Gerrit Henry

1988

Drawings on the East End: 1940–1988, The Parrish Art Museum, Southampton, NY

The Face of the Land, Southern Alleghenies Museum of Art, Loretto, PA

In Memory of John: An Exhibition in Homage to John Bernard Myers, Camillos Kouros Gallery, New York, NY

Nature in Art, One Penn Plaza, New York, NY

Still Life 88, Allport Gallery, San Francisco, CA

24th Annual Art on Paper Exhibition, Weatherspoon Art Gallery, University of North Carolina, Greensboro, NC

1987

A Just Temper Between Propensities, Bayly Art Museum, University of Virginia, Charlottesville, VA

Contemporary Still Life, Vault Gallery, Boston, MA, organized by the Art Advisory Service of the Museum of Modern Art, New York, NY

Still Life, Tibor de Nagy Gallery, New York, NY

Still Life Painting, University Gallery, University of Massachusetts, Amherst, MA

1986–87

Contemporary Romantic Landscape Painting, Orlando Museum of Art at Loch Haven, Orlando, FL

1986

Interiors in Paint, One Penn Plaza, New York, NY, curated by Gerrit Henry

Night Landscapes, Schreiber/Cutler, Inc., New York, NY

The Painterly Landscape, C. Grimaldis Gallery, Baltimore, MD

1985–86

American Art, Stamford Museum and Nature Center, Stamford, CT

The Object Revitalized, The Paine Art Center and Gardens, Oshkosh, WI

1985

The Artist Celebrates New York: Selected Paintings from The Metropolitan Museum of Art, The Metropolitian Museum of Art, New York, NY *(traveled to: Bronx Museum of the Arts, Bronx, NY; Long Island University, Brooklyn Campus, Brooklyn, NY; Jamaica Arts Center, Jamaica, NY; Staten Island Museum, Staten Island, NY; City College of New York, New York, NY)*

Contemporary American Still Life, One Penn Plaza, New York, NY, curated by Gerrit Henry

Seven Hamptons Artists, Tower Gallery, Southampton, NY

Waterworks: The Long Island Legacy, Heckscher Museum of Art, Huntington, NY

1984

Fairfield Porter: Art and Friendship, Guild Hall Museum, East Hampton, NY

(traveled to: New Britain Museum of American Art, New Britain, CT)

1983

American Still Life 1945–1983, Contemporary Arts Museum, Houston, TX *(traveled to: Albright-Knox Art Gallery, Buffalo, NY; Columbus Museum of Art, Columbus, OH; State University of New York at Purchase, NY; Portland Art Museum, Portland, OR)*

Women Painters Today, Rahr-West Art Museum, Manitowoc, WI

1982

An Appreciation of Realism, Munson-Williams-Proctor Institute, Utica, NY

Contemporary Realist Painting: A Selection, Museum of Fine Arts, Boston, MA

Eight Women / Still Life, New Britain Museum of American Art, New Britain, CT

1981

Eight with Nature, Landmark Gallery, New York, NY

Next to Nature, National Academy of Design, New York, NY

Paintings and Sculpture, Awards in Art Winners, American Academy of Arts and Letters, New York, NY

Still Life Paintings and Drawings by East End Artists, The Parrish Art Museum, Southampton, NY

1980

The Artists in the Park, Hirschl and Adler Galleries, New York, NY

The Fifties, Hirshhorn Museum and Sculpture Garden, Washington, DC

Originals, Graham Gallery, New York, NY

1979

American Academy of Arts and Letters, New York, NY

New York Now, Phoenix Art Museum, Phoenix, AZ

Painterly Realism in America, A.J. Wood Gallery, Philadelphia, PA

1978

College of William and Mary, Williamsburg, VA

Painterly Realism, Watson/de Nagy Gallery, Houston, TX

Survey of Realism, Wilkes College, Wilkes-Barre, PA

1977

American Painterly Realists, University of Missouri–Kansas City Gallery of Art, Kansas City, MO

Selected Artists, Mulvane Art Center, Topeka, KS

Still Life, Glassboro State College, Glassboro, NJ

25th Anniversary, Tibor de Nagy Gallery, New York, NY

Wish I Were There, Fendrick Gallery, Washington, DC

1975

American Academy of Arts and Letters, New York, NY

1974

New Images, The Queens Museum of Art, Queens, NY

1973

American Academy of Arts and Letters, New York, NY

Works on Paper, Baltimore Museum of Art, Baltimore, MD

1972

American Women of the 20th Century, Lakeview Museum of Arts and Sciences, Peoria, IL

A Sense of Place, Guild Hall Museum, East Hampton, NY

The Realist Revival, New York Cultural Center, New York, NY

61st Annual, Randolph-Macon College, Ashland, VA

1970

The New Landscape, Heckscher Art Museum, Huntington, NY

The Representational Spirit, State University of New York at New Paltz, NY

1969

State University of New York at New Paltz, NY

University of Iowa, Iowa City, IA

1968

Newport Festival of the Arts, Newport, RI

1967

New York Parks Commission, New York, NY

Smithsonian Institution Traveling Exhibition

1966

Hartford Arts Foundation, Hartford, CT

1965–66

Contemporary Flower Painting, The Parrish Art Museum, Southampton, NY

1965

Albright-Knox Art Gallery, Buffalo, NY

Landscape Painters, The Museum of Modern Art, New York, NY

The Newark Museum, Newark, NJ

1964–65

The Marion Koogler McNay Art Museum, San Antonio, TX

1964

Mulvane Art Center, Topeka, KS

University of Nebraska, Lincoln, NE

1963–64

The Dayton Art Institute, Dayton, OH

1963

Corcoran Gallery, Washington, DC

Landscape in Recent American Painting, The New School for Social Research, New York, NY

100 American Drawings, Phoenix Art Museum, Phoenix, AZ

1962

100 American Drawings from the Paul Magriel Collection, Lyman Allyn Museum, Massachusetts Institute of Technology, Cambridge, MA; Smithsonian Institution, Washington, DC; St. Louis Artists' Guild, St. Louis, MO

1961–63

Whitney Museum of American Art, New York, NY

1959–61

Museum of Modern Art, New York, NY

1955–57

New Talent, Museum of Modern Art Traveling Exhibition, Spoleto, Italy

1948

Pomona Museum, Pomona, CA

1947

Chicago Art Institute, Chicago, IL

Philadelphia Print Club, Philadelphia, PA

SELECTED BOOKS AND CATALOGUES

1999

Pisano, Ronald G. *Jane Wilson*. Exhib. cat., DC Moore Gallery, New York, NY.

1997

Sante, Luc. *Jane Wilson, "The Sky's Biographer."* Exhib. cat., Fischbach Gallery, New York, NY.

1996

Kertess, Klaus. *Jane Wilson Paintings: 1985–1995, "Painting the Elements."* Exhib. cat., The Parrish Art Museum, Southampton, NY.

Wasserstein, Wendy. *Jane Wilson: Watercolors.* Exhib. cat., Glenn Horowitz Bookseller, Inc., East Hampton, NY.

1995

Als, Hilton. *Jane Wilson, "It Will Soon Be Here."* Exhib. cat., Fischbach Gallery, New York, NY.

Heller, Jules, and Nancy G. Heller, eds. *North American Women Artists of the Twentieth Century: A Biographical Dictionary.* New York, NY: Garland.

Sterns, Robert A.M., Thomas Mellins, and David Fishman. *New York 1960: Architecture and Urbanism Between the Second World War and the Bicentennial.* New York, NY: Monacelli Press.

1993

Arthur, John. *Still Life: 1963–1993.* Exhib. cat., Gerald Peters Gallery, Santa Fe, NM.

Ash, John. *Jane Wilson "Jane Wilson's Northern Lights."* Exhib. cat., Fischbach Gallery, New York, NY, and Arnot Art Museum, Elmira, NY.

Esten, John. *Hampton Style.* Boston, MA: Little, Brown.

1991

Contemporary Women Artists. San Raphael, CA: Cedco Publishing.

Jane Wilson. Exhib. cat., Jaffe-Friede and Strauss Galleries, Dartmouth College, Hanover, NH.

Arthur, John. *American Realism and Figurative Art: 1952–1991.* Exhib. cat., Miyagi Museum of Art and the Japan Association of Art Museums.

Kuspit, Donald. *Jane Wilson, "Innocent Nature: Jane Wilson's Seascapes."* Exhib. cat., Fischbach Gallery, New York, NY.

1990

Frank, Elizabeth. *Jane Wilson. "Jane Wilson's American Light."* Exhib. cat., Fischbach Gallery, New York, NY

Lynes, Russel, William Gertz, and Donald Kuspit. *At the Water's Edge: 19th and 20th Century American Beach Scenes.* Tampa Museum of Art, Tampa, FL.

Pisano, Ronald C. *Long Island Landscape Painting, Volume II: The Twentieth Century.* Boston, MA: Little, Brown.

Smith, Margaret Denton. *Jane Wilson: Landscape and Still Life 1960–1990.* Exhib. cat., Marsh Gallery, University of Richmond, Richmond, VA.

1988

Beckett, Wendy. *Contemporary Women Artists.* Oxford: Phaidon.

Kertess, Klaus. *Drawings on the East End.* The Parrish Art Museum, Southampton, NY.

1983

Cathcart, Linda L. *American Still Life 1945–1983.* Houston, TX: Contemporary Arts Museum; New York, NY: Harper & Row.

1982

Rubenstein, Charlotte Streifer. *American Women Artists: From the Indian to the Present.* New York, NY: Avon; Boston, MA: G.K. Hall.

1980

Novak, Barbara, and Annette Blaugrund. *Next to Nature: Landscape Paintings from the National Academy of Design.* National Academy of Design, New York, NY

Rosenzweig, Phyllis. *Art of the Fifties: Aspects of Painting in New York.* Washington, DC: The Hirshhorn Museum and Sculpture Garden, The Smithsonian Institution, Washington, DC.

1979

Munro, Eleanor. *Originals: American Women Artists.* New York, NY: Simon and Schuster.

1978

Meyer, Susan, ed. *20 Oil Painters and How They Work.* New York, NY: Watson-Guptill.

1977

Bard, Joellen, Dore Ashton, and Lawrence Alloway. *Tenth Street Days, The Co-ops of the Fifties.* New York, NY: Education, Art & Service, Inc.

1972

Coke, Van Deren. *The Painter and the Photograph: From Delacroix to Warhol.* Albuquerque, NM: University of New Mexico Press

Gruen, John. *The Party's Over Now: Reminiscences of the Fifties.* New York, NY: Viking Press.

1971

Gussow, Alan. *A Sense of Place: The Artist and the American Land.* San Francisco, CA: Friends of the Earth; New York, NY: Saturday Review Press.

1967

Berkson, Bill, ed. *In Memory of My Feelings/A Selection of Poems by Frank O'Hara.* New York, NY: The Museum of Modern Art.

1955

Logan, John. *Cycle for Mother Cabrini.* Signed special edition of 26 with original block prints by the artist. New York, NY: Grove Press.

SELECTED PERIODICALS

1999

Braff, Phyllis. "Diverse Views of a Changing Landscape," *The New York Times*, May 23.

McDonough, Tom. "Jane Wilson at DC Moore," *Art in America*, October.

Naves, Mario. "Full-bodied Skyscapes That Hardly Hold Paint," *The New York Observer*, May 1.

1998

Gardner, Paul. "Taking the Plunge," *ARTnews*, February.

Kuspit, Donald. "Jane Wilson at Fischbach," *Artforum*, February.

1997

Nahas, Dominique. "Jane Wilson at Fischbach," *Review*, November 1.

1996

Braff, Phyllis. "Long Island Landscape: A New Era," *The New York Times*, September 11.

Cross, Jennifer. "At the Parrish: 2 Compelling Shows," *The Southampton Press*, May 23.

Cummings, Mary. "Jane Wilson Works Are All About Light," *The Southampton Press*, July 4.

Duncan, Erika. "Appreciating Beauty of Time and Place Translated into Color," *The New York Times*, May 12.

Glueck, Grace. "City Sophistication Spends the Summer on Long Island," *The New York Times*, July 12.

Kimmelman, Michael. "Where Art Thrives Beyond New York City," *The New York Times*, July 12.

Little, Carl. "Jane Wilson at The Parrish Art Museum," *Art in America*, November.

Lovelace, Carey. "The East End Light," *Newsday*, May 24.

Saltz, Jerry. "A Year in the Life: Tropic of Painting," *Art in America*, October.

Slivka, Rose. "Wilson at Parrish Art Museum," *The East Hampton Star*, May 23.

Smith, Roberta. *The New York Times*, March 25.

Stevens, Mark. "The Way We Were," *New York*, July 8.

Weiss, Mary Wolberg. "Jane Wilson At The Parrish," *Dan's Paper*, June 28.

1993

Cotter, Holland. "Wilson at Fischbach," *The New York Times*, October 15.

Pozzi, Lucio. "Che ve ne sembra dell America? Lettera da New York," *Il Giornale Dell'arte*, no. 116, November.

1992

Cohen, Ronny. "Wilson at Fischbach," *Artforum*, March.

"Jane Wilson Honored," *The East Hampton Star*, May 21.

Pagel, David. "Light in Landscapes," *Los Angeles Times*, August 7.

"Spectrum," *ARTnews*, Summer.

1991

Hammond, Pamela. "Wilson at Earl McGrath Gallery," *ARTnews*, March.

Hurwitz, Laurie S. "Jane Wilson," *American Artist*, June.

Kramer, Hilton. "Wilson at Fischbach," *The New York Observer*, November 18.

McRenna, Kristine. "Sky Lights," *Los Angeles Times*, January 1.

Thompson, Mimi. "Jane Wilson," *Bomb*, Fall.

1990

Ash, John. "Wilson at Fischbach," *Art in America*, October.

1989

Solomon, Mike. "Strong Benton Show," *The East Hampton Star*, August 24.

1988

Artner, Alan G. "Wilson at Compass Rose Gallery," *The Chicago Tribune*, January 29.

Bass, Ruth. "Wilson at Fischbach," *ARTnews*, September.

1986

Henry, Gerrit. "Jane Wilson at Fischbach," *Art in America*, March.

1985

Gardner, Paul. "Jane Wilson's Weather Eye," *ARTnews*, December.

1984

Brenson, Michael. "Wilson at Fischbach," *The New York Times*, February 24.

"Contemporary Artists at the Met," *Travel and Leisure*, February.

Henry, Gerrit. "Wilson at Fischbach," *ARTnews*, May.

Raynor, Vivien. "Painting by 15 Friends of Fairfield Porter," *The New York Times*, August 3.

1981

Bass, Ruth. "Some Kind of Wrestling Match," *ARTnews*, October.

Harrison, Helen A. "Lively Experiments with Still Life," *The New York Times*, May 3.

Kakutani, Michiko. "Guild Hall and the Greening of East Hampton," *The New York Times*, June 7.

1979

Braff, Phyllis. "From the Studio," *The East Hampton Star*, August 2.

Harrison, Helen A. "Homage Paid to South Fork," *The New York Times*, July 29.

Preston, Malcomb. "Art: The South Fork Light," *Newsday*, August 8.

1974

Cochraine, Diane. "Remembrance of Images Past and Present," *American Artist*, December.

1973

Mellow, James. "Art: Unusual Still Lives," *The New York Times*, April 14.

1971

Campbell, Lawrence. *ARTnews*, April.

Canaday, John. *The New York Times*, April 24.

Mellow James R. "New Life in the Nude and the Still Life," *The New York Times*, April.

1969

Campbell, Lawrence. *ARTnews*, December.

1965

Golden, Amy. *Arts*, September.

1964

Artforum, April.

Art in America, August.

1963

Campbell, Lawrence. *ARTnews*, Summer.

Canaday, John. "Jane Wilson: A Sweet Problem," *The New York Times*, May 12.

1962

Campbell, Lawrence. *ARTnews*, Summer.

"New Blood." *ARTnews*, January.

1961

Canaday, John. "Art: The Whitney Annual," *The New York Times*, December 13.

Tenke, Lois. "Couple Practices Artistic Togetherness," *Newsday*, October 12.

1960

Ashton, Dore. *The New York Times*, May.

1959

Porter, Fairfield. *ARTnews*, April.

1958
Campbell, Lawrence. *ARTnews*, April.

1957
"Women Artists in Ascendance," *Life Magazine*, May 13.
Y., V. *Arts*, February.

1955
Ashton, Dore. "About Art and Artists," *The New York Times*, October 27.
ARTnews, November.

1953
G., B. *ARTnews*, November.

AWARDS

1993
The Lotus Club Medal of Merit, New York, NY

1990
Benjamin Altman Prize, National Academy of Design, New York, NY

1988
The Eloise Spaeth Award for Distinguished Achievement in Painting, Guild Hall Museum, East Hampton, NY

1987
Adolph and Clara Obrig Prize, National Academy of Design, New York, NY

1985
Adolph and Clara Obrig Prize, National Academy of Design, New York, NY
Award in Art, American Academy of Arts and Letters, New York, NY

1981
Childe Hassam Purchase Fund, American Academy of Arts and Letters, New York, NY

1977
Ranger Purchase Prize, National Academy of Design, New York, NY

1973
Childe Hassam Purchase Fund, American Academy of Arts and Letters, New York, NY

1972
Childe Hassam Purchase Fund, American Academy of Arts and Letters, New York, NY

1967
Louis Comfort Tiffany Foundation, New York, NY

1963
Ingram Merrill Foundation, New York, NY

MEMBERSHIPS

American Academy of Arts and Letters, New York, NY, 1991
National Academy of Design, New York, NY, 1975
Council, 1980–86, 1989–94
President, 1992–94
Skowhegan School of Painting and Sculpture, Skowhegan, ME
Board of Governors, 1981–90
Chair, 1984–86

SELECTED CORPORATE COLLECTIONS

Allied Bank, Dallas, TX
American Telephone and Telegraph, New York, NY
Ashland Oil Company, Ashland, KY
Banctexas, Dallas, TX
Carnegie Corporation, New York, NY
Chase Manhattan Bank, New York, NY
CIGNA, Philadelphia, PA
Citibank, New York, NY
Commerce Bancshares, Inc. Kansas City, MO
Debevoise and Plimpton, New York, NY
First Interstate Bank, Dallas, TX
General Atlantic Partners, Greenwich, CT
Little Caesar Enterprises, Inc., Detroit, MI
The Long Term Credit Bank of Japan, Ltd., New York, NY
Main-Hurdman Collection, New York, NY
Marsh & McLennan Companies, New York, NY
The Metropolitan Life Insurance Company, New York, NY
The National Bank of Commerce, Dallas, TX
Neuberger and Berman, New York, NY
Newport News Shipbuilding and Drydock, Norfolk, VA
Norton and Company, New York, NY
NTC Group, Inc., Greenwich, CT
Parker Pen Corporation, Janesville, WI
The Prudential, New York, NY
Singer Sewing Machine Company of Canada, Ltd., Quebec
Spears, Benzak, Salomon and Farrell, Inc., New York, NY
Stroock, Stroock and Lavan, New York, NY
Towers Parrin, New York, NY
The Uris Corporation, New York, NY
Yasuda Fire and Marine Insurance Company, New York, NY
Zurich Kemper Investments, Chicago, IL

SELECTED PUBLIC COLLECTIONS

American Embassy, Manila, The Philippines
The Asheville Art Museum, Asheville, NC
Bryn Mawr College, Bryn Mawr, PA
Guild Hall Museum, East Hampton, NY
The Herron Art Institute, Cincinnati, OH
The Hirshhorn Museum and Sculpture Garden, Washington, DC
The Kalamazoo Institute of Art, Kalamazoo, MI
Kemper Museum of Contemporary Art, Kansas City, MO
The Metropolitan Museum of Art, New York, NY
Museo dell'Arte, Udine, Italy
Museum of Foreign Art, Sophia, Bulgaria
Museum of Modern Art, New York, NY
The National Academy of Design, New York, NY
The Nelson-Atkins Museum of Art, Kansas City, MO
New Orleans Museum of Art, New Orleans, LA
New York University, New York, NY
The Parrish Art Museum, Southampton, NY
The Pennsylvania Academy of Fine Art, Philadelphia, PA
Rockefeller University, New York, NY
The San Francisco Museum of Modern Art, San Francisco, CA
The Smithsonian Institution, Washington, DC
The State University of New York, Oneonta, NY
The Tampa Museum of Art, Tampa, FL
Vassar College, Poughkeepsie, NY
Wadsworth Atheneum Museum of Art, Hartford, CT
Whitney Museum of American Art, New York, NY

This exhibition and catalog are dedicated to the memory of Ronald G. Pisano (1948–2000), author, scholar, curator, and discerning collector. His unstinting advocacy of the art of Long Island, both early and contemporary, was manifested not only in his writing but also in the exhibitions he curated, and in his own collection.

HECKSCHER MUSEUM OF ART	DC MOORE GALLERY
2 Prime Avenue, Huntington, NY 11743	724 Fifth Avenue, New York, NY 10019
Telephone (631) 351-3250	Telephone (212) 247-2111
February 3 – April 15, 2001	May 8 – June 8, 2001

FRONTISPIECE: Jane Wilson in front of her painting *The Open Scene*, May 1960

FRONT ENDPAPER: Jane Wilson in her New York studio, 1999

BACK ENDPAPER: Jane Wilson at Shinto Farm, Milbrook, New York, June 2000

Copyright © 2001 DC Moore Gallery   "A Conversation with Jane Wilson" © 2001 Justin Spring   Portraits of the Artist Copyright © John Jonas Gruen

COLOR PHOTOGRAPHY: *Kevin Ryan, Jerry Thompson*   DESIGN: *John Bernstein*   PRINT PRODUCTION: *Studio Gribaudo*   PRINTING: *Pozzo Gros Monti S.p.A., Italy*

LIBRARY OF CONGRESS NUMBER: 00-112237   ISBN: 1-879195-11-9